The German Shepherd Big Book: All About The German Shepherd Breed

What Every Shepherd Owner Needs To Know About His or Her Pet

DEDICATION

I want to dedicate this book to past, present and future German Shepherd lovers everywhere.

TABLE OF CONTENTS

PUBLISHER'S NOTES

DISCLAIMER AND TERMS OF USE AGREEMENT:
(Please Read Before Using This Book)

INTRODUCTION

Bringing any new dog into your life is a big decision. If the dog is a German Shepherd the decision is even bigger–as this breed comes with a lot of horse power and responsibility.

I often hear people talking about wanting a German Shepherd because they had one as a kid, based on a Shepherd they met once, because of their looks or because of their intelligence.

Most people get caught up in the excitement of getting a new dog or puppy and don't consider the time, energy, money and commitment needed to accommodate a German Shepherd for the duration of its life.

The German Shepherd Dog is a loyal companion and can be a wonderful addition to your family if you have the time and energy to put in. When the right German Shepherd is paired with the right home or owner, the positive aspects of the breed far outweigh the negatives.

This book's goal is to help determine if a German Shepherd Dog is right for you. (This book is NOT about training your German Shepherd or correcting behavioral issues.)

If you are ready to commit to this incredible breed, this book will give some background as well as some tips, facts and knowledge that every Shepherd owner should be aware of.

Take the information from this book to help you to find the right German Shepherd to fit your needs and lifestyle.

CHAPTER 1: THE HISTORY OF THE GERMAN SHEPHERD BREED

<u>Captain Max von Stephanitz (1864–1936)</u>

The German Shepherd Dog (GSD) is known also by the titles of Alsatian and Deutscher Schäferhund, which is the German translation for the German Shepherd Dog. The GSD is a working dog that was initially developed for guarding and herding sheep. The GSD is a large size dog that was created in Germany and is a relatively new breed of purebred dogs that only dates back to 1899.

The German Shepherd is the product of Captain Max Von Stephanitz's (1864-1936) vision of creating the perfect working dog that would possess the following essential qualities: intelligence, ability, a weatherproof coat, and beauty.

During the 1800s in Europe, many attempts were made to regulate breeds of existing dogs. In Germany, shepherds chose and bred dogs that were perceived to have the characteristics required for herding sheep and protecting them from predators; some of these traits were speed, intelligence, a keen sense of smell, and strength.

Before von Stephanitz standardized the German Shepherd breed, German Shepherd Dogs were just dogs of various breeds that belonged to German shepherds. The early shepherd breeders were only interested in function and not form, thus producing dogs that were capable of performing their tasks, but the dogs' ability and appearance varied significantly from one German neighboring community to the next.

The Phylax Society was a club formed in 1891 by dog fanciers who intended to foster and standardize dog breeds in Germany. The club was short-lived and only existed into 1894. The society separated after only three years because of continuing inside disagreements over traits in the dogs that the society wished to promote. Some members believed dogs should be bred exclusively for purposes of working, while other members believed dogs should be bred for appearance.

The goal of the Phylax Society failed, but it encouraged people to standardize dog breeds independently. Because of the Phylax Society's influence, other breed clubs later emerged.

Ex-cavalry Captain Max Von Stephanitz was one Phylax Society member who strongly believed dogs should be bred for working purposes. Beauty by itself meant nothing to him; he believed it naturally followed form and utility.

On April 2, 1899 von Stephanitz attended the Karlsruhe Dog Show and purchased a four-year-old yellow and gray dog about 25 inches tall at the withers. The dog was named Hektor Linksrhein and was the invention of a few selective generations of breeding. It embodied what Von Stephanitz perceived a working dog should be. The dog's strength pleased him. He was captivated with the animal's loyalty, beauty and intelligence. Von Stephanitz renamed the dog Horand von Grafrath. (Captain von Stephanitz started the trend of using *von* within the German Shepherds name which in Germany suggests a noble ancestry.)

In 1899, von Stephanitz founded the Verein Für Fur Deutscher Schäferhund (Club for German Shepherd Dogs), or simply the SV. That same year, the SV approved a breed standard, and the world's oldest German Shepherd registry was opened. Horand von Grafrath became the foundation dog of the German Shepherd Dog Breed and was the first registered German Shepherd Dog whose official number was SZ1.

V Horand von Grafrath (Hektor Linksrhein)

Verein Für Fur Deutscher Schäferhund held conformation shows, known as Sieger, where dogs were rated G (good), SG (very good), V (excellent), or VA (excellent select). To be allowed to breed, a dog had to be rated and have a hip certification. For a litter to be registered in Germany, both parents had to have at least a G (good) conformation rating and working titles (Schutzhund).

A Schutzhund (protection dog) title has three parts, including obedience, tracking and protection. Schutzhund demonstrates a dog's ability to work, and a dog must be proficient in all three parts to earn a Schutzhund title. Von Stephanitz made the Schutzhund title a requirement in order for SV club members to breed and register their dogs.

Von Stephanitz controlled the SV with an iron fist as the founder, first president and self-appointed breeding master, judge, and breed inspector. Von Stephanitz wrote of the German Shepherd Dog standard as from his own vision of the perfect, highly efficient herding dog:-"A pleasing appearance is desirable, but it cannot put the dog's working ability into question." He sought a dog "firm of nerve, attentiveness, unshockability, tractability, watchfulness, reliability, and incorruptibility together with courage, fighting tenacity, and hardness." Von Stephanitz's ultimate GSD evolved into, "utility and intelligence."

As the twentieth century approached, von Stephanitz realized that the German Shepherds original job of sheepherding was rapidly disappearing as fences were erected and rail travel became an efficient way to transport livestock. Herding dogs were no longer needed in great numbers, and some herding breeds vanished.

Von Stephanitz felt that his beloved breed had the potential to do other kinds of work and he was right. At the time of this publication, the German Shepherd Dog has proven capable of assuming many of the different roles listed below:

- Bomb Detection Dog
- Cadaver Dog
- Companion Dog
- Drug Detection Dog
- Family Pet
- Guard Dog
- Guide Dog for the Blind
- Hearing Dog for the Deaf
- Herding Dog
- Man/Women's best friend
- Military Dog

- Mobility Assistance Dog (owners in wheelchairs)
- Movie star
- Obedience Dog
- Police Dog
- Search and Rescue Dog (SAR)
- Seizure Alert Dogs
- Service Dog (assisting owner with everyday tasks)
- Show Dog
- Therapy Dog
- Tracking Dog
- TV actor

Herding Dog

The German Shepherd Dog descended from herding dogs and today they are still classified by the American Kennel Club as a herding breed.

Centuries ago the German Shepherd was first utilized as a herding dog, but varied from other herding breeds. The early German Shepherd Dog would guard its flock or herd throughout the day and confine the animals being guarded from entering or leaving the selected area. The German Shepherd Dog was not only asked to "tend" the sheep but also to protect them from wolves, bears and enterprising humans.

The instincts that make a good herding dog are still presently found in many German Shepherds who have never met a sheep. German Shepherds instinctively follow their intuition to protect their flock or family from harm. This intuition is one factor that makes this breed an outstanding guard dog. A good herding dog will instinctively run a circle around the flock, herd, family or kids to keep them in a specific area, field or front yard. Even today, if allowed, German Shepherds will often try to "guide" or "direct" you or your family to ensure you are safe. Teach an attentive German Shepherd what his boundaries are and let him constructively use his instincts to protect his family and home.

War Dog

World War I

The German army began World War I with 6,000 trained military dogs, many of which were German Shepherds. By the end of the war it was estimated that more than a million dogs served on both sides.

German Shepherds were used in many capacities during the war. They delivered messages to maintain communications and transported ammunition and medical supplies (also known as Red Cross dogs, comfort dogs, or Sanitätshunde). Messenger dogs were valued for their loyalty.

Shepherds also guarded and herded livestock that was kept near the front lines for the German army.

The German Shepherd was best known as a sentry (stationary alert) and a scout (moving alert). Sentries were trained to alert their handlers to someone approaching by growling or barking. Sentries proved to be very valuable at night in case of attack under cover of darkness. Scouts were used for the same skills as sentry dogs but were trained to work in silence in order to assist with the detection of snipers, ambushes and other enemy forces.

German Shepherds were also used to patrol prison camps to prevent prisoners from escaping or communicating with their comrades.

World War II

U.S. Marines December 1943

When World War II began, Germany was estimated to have more than 200,000 trained military and police dogs, mostly German Shepherds.

In the United States, training dogs for military purposes was mostly abandoned after World War I. When the country entered World War II in December 1941 the American Kennel Association and a group called Dogs for Defense encouraged dog owners to donate healthy and capable animals to the Quartermaster Corps (QMC) of the U.S. Army for the newly established War Dog Program, or "K-9 Corps." The K-9 Corps initially took over 30 breeds of dogs, but by the fall of 1944 the list of preferred breeds was narrowed to seven: German Shepherds, Belgian Sheep Dogs, Doberman Pinschers, Collies, Siberian Huskies, Malamutes and Eskimo dogs. Mixed crosses of these breeds were also acceptable.

By 1945 the Army Quartermaster Corps had trained almost 10,000 dogs for the Army, Navy Marine Corps and Coast Guard. Fifteen War Dog platoons served overseas in World War II.

As in World War I, dogs were again used to transport food and medical supplies, to work as sentries, scouts, messengers, search and rescue dogs, and mine dogs. Mine dogs were also called M-dogs or mine detection dogs. Mine dogs were trained to sniff out enemy ambushes such as booby traps, trip wires, and mines.

Chip, a German Shepherd who served with the Army's 3rd Infantry Division was the top canine hero of World War II. Chip was trained as a sentry. He broke away from his handler and attacked an enemy machine gun nest in Italy, forcing the entire enemy crew to surrender. Chip was wounded in the attack but was awarded the Distinguished Service Cross, Silver Star and the Purple Heart. (All awards were later revoked due to an Army policy preventing official commendation of animals.)

Post-World War II

When World War II ended, the American military downsized its military dog program. In 1951, the Military Police Corps assumed the responsibility of training military dogs.

That same year, U.S. dog platoons were activated when aggression broke out in Korea. The dog platoons, consisting primarily of German Shepherds, were very successful.

From 1960 to 1975, German Shepherds were primarily utilized in the U.S. Military as patrol and sentry dogs. 1965 marked the first time military dog teams were sent to Vietnam.

Dogs continued to serve the armed forces with distinction in Desert Storm, Afghanistan and Iraq.

Today's military dog is multifaceted, and is trained as a dual-purpose dog. Today's modern German Shepherd is trained as a patrol dog and narcotics or explosive detection dog. German Shepherds easily handle multiple tasks because of their versatility and intelligence.

The German Shepherd Dog has played an important role in our military's past and will undoubtedly continue to faithfully serve and protect our country's current and future soldiers.

Service Dog

It is rumored that von Stephanitz had to beg German police departments to take a chance on his beloved breed for police work. Von Stephanitz's perseverance and the German Shepherds all around excellence eventually won over the German police and departments soon found the dogs to be invaluable law enforcement partners. For many years, the German Shepherd was simply referred to as the "German Police Dogs."

The German Shepherd has been the top choice in the United States for police and service work for more than a half century. The German Shepherd Dog is athletic, versatile, intelligent, fearless, loyal, strong, intimidating, can exert up to 1,200 pounds of bite pressure per square inch.

They have an excellent sense of smell, and want to work and please their handler. Other breeds come and go in popularity, but departments that stray from the German Shepherd K9 Officer, eventually return.

German Shepherds also serve many government agencies such as the U.S. Department of Agriculture, the Bureau of Alcohol, Tobacco and Firearms, U.S. Border Patrol, the Federal Bureau of Investigation, the Central Intelligence Agency, the National Transportation Safety Board, the U.S. State Department, state and federal penitentiaries, etc.

Countless military dogs and K9 officers are hero's for sacrificing their own lives to save the lives of so many, whether it has been on the front lines of battle, or fighting crime to make our cities and neighborhoods safe.

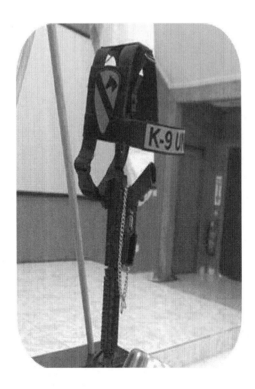

CHAPTER 2: AM I READY TO OWN A GERMAN SHEPHERD DOG?

The German Shepherd enjoys a universal admiration and hero worship that is well deserved. They are easily one of the most widely accepted and recognized breeds of dog anywhere in the world. They are known for remarkable courage, loyalty, and the ability to work in virtually any situation with intelligence and an unparalleled eagerness to please.

Know that the breed is not for everyone. There are advantages and pitfalls to living with a big, smart, active dog.

If you are considering adding a German Shepherd to your family you need to understand the time, energy, and money required on your part when committing to this breed.

Time

Most breeds want attention but German Shepherds demand it, and lots of it.

German Shepherds do not react well to be being left alone for excessive periods of time. Leaving this breed out in the yard, isolated from you the family and deprived of interaction, love and attention will result in behavioral issues. Issues to expect range from digging, excessive barking, destructive chewing, escaping your yard, separation anxiety, aggression, etc.

If you work long hours and travel frequently, a German Shepherd will not thrive.

My current German Shepherd is 16 months old. I work 40 hours a week and leave him kenneled in an outside run when I am at work. He wears a bark collar when kenneled outside to prevent nuisance (boredom) barking and to keep him from annoying the retired neighbors.

When running short errands after work or on the weekends, I usually kennel him in a crate within the house. As he matures, he earns more trust, freedom and privileges. Eventually, he will be given free rein of the house when home alone. Kenneling and crating is how I control my German Shepherd from becoming a "German shredder" and developing unwanted behavioral issues.

When I return home from a long day at work, or any extended amount of time that has resulted in my pup kenneled and by himself, the first hour home is quality time spent playing and interacting with my puppy. This time is a must to enforce obedience and manners through play, and to burn off pent up energy.

Whenever I am home, my German Shepherd is never very far from my side. Where I go, he follows. German Shepherds are pack animals and they are all about interaction. They want to be with you, their family members or their "pack." I happen to enjoy this watchfulness and companionship.

The German Shepherd Dog requires human companionship, lots of socialization, and a lot of training, as well as mental and physical stimulation. German Shepherds are exceptionally intelligent and their minds need as much exercise as their bodies. If you do not keep a German Shepherd mentally stimulated, they will become bored and entertain themselves through potentially destructive and undesirable behavior.

German Shepherds need pack structure. As the owner of a German Shepherd, you must establish leadership and set boundaries early on. If you do not establish yourself as the Alpha of the pack and earn the respect of a German Shepherd, a German Shepherd will lead you, dominate you and run you and your household.

If you are thinking about getting a German Shepherd puppy, you need to understand the extra time commitment they require. They need socialization, socialization and socialization—socialization that includes exposure to new places, loud noises, everyday sounds and noises, strangers, other dogs and animals.

Obedience is not an option with this breed. Socialization, obedience and keeping your German Shepherd active does not end with puppyhood. It is ongoing throughout the dog's life. A German Shepherd puppy is a full time job, on top of your full time job, and they are puppies until the age of two. Some dogs are slow to mature and may remain very puppy-like until the age of four or five.

Energy

If you are a couch potato and do not plan on becoming physically active, you may want to reconsider bringing home a German Shepherd.

German Shepherds need human interaction, which means that they want to be with YOU. They want to be active with you and they want their physical exercise to include you. A German Shepherd owner needs the same level of energy (or more) to match the energy level of the German Shepherd Dog.

German Shepherds were bred to be on the move and cover miles and miles of territory per day. They are working dogs, and they mentally and physically need to have a job to feel they are a contributing member of your family or lifestyle.

Do not over think jobs for your German Shepherd. German Shepherds are instinctively a protective breed. Protecting you, your family and your property is a job, and a job they are very good at. Send your German Shepherd outside with the kids to play and they will keep a watchful eye over them. Jobs can also be simple and fun. Hide your dog's toys and teach him to search for them. Anything that will keep your shepherd mentally stimulated, physically active or included in the family "pack" structure will keep a German Shepherd content and busy. With this breed, a tired dog is a fulfilled and happy dog.

An active German Shepherd makes a better overall companion. There are a ton of activities that German Shepherds enjoy and excel at. Some are structured and competitive, and some are just fun.

Here are some activities to look into:
- Agility
- Canine Good Citizen
- Certified Therapy Dog
- Competition Obedience
- Confirmation
- Dock Jumping
- Fly Ball

- Freestyle Obedience
- Herding
- Hiking
- KNVP
- Personal Protection Sport Clubs
- Rally Obedience
- Ring Sport
- Schutzhund
- Search and Rescue
- Swimming
- Tracking

Most of the activities listed require time, energy and commitment on your part. Your participation is mandatory, and you and your German Shepherd will become a team working together. Working a German Shepherd is a rewarding experience that builds trust and an unspoken bond.

Money

Big dogs simply cost more to own than small dogs. They eat more food, need larger supplies and equipment, and require larger doses of medicine or vaccinations at vet visits.

The average life span for this dog is anywhere between ten to fifteen years, which means committing to the financial care and well-being of this pet for a considerable amount of time.

Can you afford a German Shepherd? Below is a list of needs and expenses you should be aware of:

- Purchase price of dog or puppy
- Puppy vaccinations
- Yearly vaccinations/check-ups/preventative care
- Neuter/spay
- Fencing
- Outside kennel
- Plastic crate/wire crate
- City or county dog license
- Collar and tags
- Leash & other misc. training equipment
- Toys

- Food & water dishes
- Food & treats
- Grooming tools/grooming expenses
- Training classes
- Specialized training/sport work - fees & equipment
- Boarding fees if you travel
- Replacement of clothing/carpet/furniture/landscaping/etc.
- Bigger yard, bed and vehicle

This list of expenses can be incurred with any breed but keep in mind that the bigger your breed is, the bigger your bills will be.

Traits

The characteristics, traits and energy of the German Shepherd Dog that may be considered negative qualities for some people are positive qualities for others.

Smart dogs can be a handful. On the plus side, smart dogs are easy to train because they are eager to learn, and they learn quickly. A German Shepherd will quickly pick up the daily routines and habits of their owners.

German Shepherds are energetic by nature. They want to spend time with their humans and they are instinctively protective. With proper training, this makes them the perfect companion to accompany you on a walk, jog, hike or camping trip.

The German Shepherd's protective instincts come from his early herding background. With no flock to protect, the German Shepherd will protect its people and their property.

The German Shepherd's naturally protective instincts mean that they do not greet every person they meet with a sloppy tongue and a wagging tail. A German Shepherd will stand its ground, look people in the eye and size them up. Friendly strangers may be greeted with a tail that is cautious to wag. Strange or threatening people will be greeted, at a minimum, with a low warning growl. Known friends and family will be remembered, recognized and greeted as welcomed guests.

Set some boundaries, give some positive reinforcement, and sleep a little easier knowing the resident shepherd is on duty as the full time guard dog watching over you, your family, your house and your property.

The German Shepherd Dog is a versatile breed that wants to be useful and please its owners. A shepherd's personality can be serious and intimidating, but these dogs are also very playful and expressive. Regardless of the role you want a Shepherd to take—working dog, sport dog, family dog, companionship, watchdog, sleeping buddy—a German Shepherd can perform them all and fill a void in your life that you never knew was missing with their love, devotion, loyalty, and playful antics.

When German Shepherds are paired with the right owners, they are outstanding companions. Their loyalty and love is fierce and their hearts are huge. When this breed commits to something or someone, they wholeheartedly commit 100%. When a German Shepherd protects its family, searches for a missing person, chases a stick, snores on the couch, or hogs the bed, he goes big and he goes all out. If you are lucky enough to have a German Shepherd love you, it will love you with everything it has.

CHAPTER 3: GERMAN SHEPHERD BREED STANDARDS – SIZE, CHARACTERISTICS, COATS & COLORS

Size

The modern German Shepherd is an athletic medium to large-sized breed that is athletic, strong, well-muscled and has an overall proportionate and balanced appearance.

The German Shepherd Dog is one breed that should definitively look masculine or feminine. Males are taller, heavier and squarer through the face. Females are shorter, lighter and narrower through the face and muzzle area.

The Breed Standard dictates the following ideal height and weight requirement for a GSD:

Males

23–26 inches (60–65 cm) tall at the withers
Weight between 66–88 lbs. (30-40 kg)

Females

21-24 inches (55-60 cm) tall at the withers
Weight between 49–71 lbs. (22-32 kg)

* Height and weight is approximate

The standard calls for the above heights and weights to help keep the GSD built for work, health, longevity and performance. The standard size German Shepherd will be more athletic, have more endurance, have fewer joint issues due to weight, be a better sport or working dog and have an easier time just getting around in general.

Characteristics

The German Shepherd Dog should be well-balanced, firm in nerves, self-confident, absolutely calm and impartial, and (except in tempting situations) amiable. He must possess courage, willingness to fight, and hardness in order to be suitable as a companion, watchdog, protector, service dog, and guardian.

They have a wedge-shaped head that is large but in proportion to the body and a forehead that is domed; these dogs have an elongated square-cut muzzle with lips that are tight against the teeth and dark in color, and a nose that is large, wide and black.

The jaws on these dogs are strong; they have a bite that can be compared with a scissor-like cut. The eyes of the German Shepherd are medium in size, almond-shaped and sparkling brown with a clever look that is self-assured.

The ears are normally large and always stand erect; they are normally open at the front and parallel, but are frequently pulled back throughout movement. The necks on these dogs are long, and it is lifted up when they become excited, lowered when moving at a fast pace. The German Shepherd's tail is bushy and fairly long. The shoulders slope into a straight, strong back and movement is effortless and long, with a smooth trot.

Coat Types

The German Shepherd breed has three coat variations according to the WUSV (World Union of German Shepherd Dog Clubs). They are:

1. Stock Coat
2. Long Stock Coat
3. Long Hair

Stock Coat

The stock coat is the most common and familiar coat on the German Shepherd Dog. This is the desired coat according to the standard and can vary from a very short fur to a plushier, thicker fur.

Long Stock Coat

This coat is most often referred to as a "coat" "coated" or "long coat." A "long coat" has longer, fluffier fur with a thick undercoat. They usually have fluffy fur around their ears and on the back of their legs, and are usually beautiful animals. Some German Shepherd owners prefer the appearance of a coated shepherd over a stock coat Shepherd.

The long coat gene is a simple recessive gene, thus making coated dogs somewhat rarer. Both parents are required to be coated or carry the recessive gene in order to produce long coated puppies. Even after many years of carefully planned breeding, a few coated puppies are occasionally born into a stock coat litter. Hard core breeders are not happy when a coated puppy appears in a litter and will try to breed this out of their kennel's bloodline.

Long hair puppies pop up from two stock coated dogs because each parent is carrying the recessive gene. A lot of breeders will not breed these two dogs again. Both of these dogs could be bred to different mates who do not carry the gene, and both could potentially produce litters without any coated offspring.

As a buyer, a coated puppy can be an indication that the whole litter is going to be a good one. This is because the sires and dams who have produced the litter are carriers of strong genetics from their ancestors. Puppies with this recessive gene generally have a strong-boned body structure, are exceptionally good-natured, and are of sound character.

There is no correlation between a dog's coat and working ability. It is not uncommon to see police and military service dogs that are coated. This is because the coated shepherd can be purchased for less money–yet it still has the genetics, heart and drive to fill the requirements of the job and the handler.

My first German Shepherd, Hannibal, was coated. I purchased him from a local reputable breeder. It was obvious at only eight weeks of age he was going to be a coat due to the fact he was fuzzier than his siblings. The breeder explained that the longer coat was considered a breed fault, but if I was not interested in breeding or showing (which I was not), he would be a loyal family addition. I took the little ball of fur home for less than half of what his littermates were going for and he was a fantastic dog.

Hannibal

A German Shepherd's coat length boils down to personal preferences. I have not had another coated shepherd since Hannibal, but I would not hesitate to own another one. Just be prepared to defend your coated German Shepherd's heritage, as a lot of people will mistake it for a mixed breed or a wolf hybrid.

Long Hair

A true "long hair" coated German Shepherd Dog is very rare. It has longer silky fur with no undercoat. The hair parts down the middle of the back and flows down the sides of the dog. Most people have never seen or heard of this rare coat.

Perception of the long coated shepherd varies across standards; AKC deems them as faulty. Long coats are recognized under the German Kennel Club and the United Kingdom Kennel Club. The WUSV/SV has approved long stock coat dogs to be bred and shown. In the past they were allowed to participate in Schutzhund, but were disqualified from the show ring and breeding.

Regardless of region or organization, a German Shepherd dog is disqualified from breeding if there is no undercoat.

The Many Colors of the GSD

The German Shepherd dog comes in a variety of colors. The breed standard calls for nice dark pigment and rich colors. Colors that are considered "disqualifying" or "undesirable" according to the German Shepherd Dog standard are white, blue and liver. All others are considered "correct color."

In some breeds certain colors are connected to specific health issues, but this is not the case within the German Shepherd Dog breed.

Rumors that white, blue and liver dogs will have a higher occurrence of health problems are unfounded and based on misconceptions and incorrect information. These Shepherds are no more likely to have health problems than any other color Shepherd.

Never choose a German Shepherd based on color alone. While you may have a color preference, please look for more important traits such as health, temperament, working ability, and structure.

Let's take a look at the many colors of the German Shepherd Dog.

Black & Tan

The black and tan is the most common color in the breed and what the average person envisions when they think of the German Shepherd breed.

There are many color variations within the black and tan color. The tan color can range from a deep rich red to a light pale silver color. The pattern of black can range from a saddle back to blanket back. A saddle back is just what it sounds like: the black color looks like a saddle over the dogs back and sides. A blanket back is darker in color and the black covers more of the dog's back and sides. Some black and tan dogs have very little black covering their backs.

Black and tan is recessive to the most dominant sable gene, but it is dominant over the solid black recessive gene. Black and tan dogs are generally born darker and lighten up as they mature. The black will recede and the tan will become more prominent. It is not uncommon for some black and tans (especially females) to develop a grey strip down their back;

this is often called a "bitch's strip."

West German show lines are commonly black and red. Black and tans and bicolors are found more in the various working lines.

Sable

The most dominant color in the German Shepherd breed is a sable color. Most people are not familiar with a sable German Shepherd; they are used to seeing the typical black and tan variety.

Sable dogs often have a color pattern that looks similar to a grey wolf. If you examine a single hair from a sable dog you will commonly see two or three different colors on the strand of hair.

Sable dogs can range in color from a very light grey or tan to a darker, richer red or grey color to a dark brown or black color. All shades of sable are acceptable but dark pigment is preferred. Lighter sables lack pigment, causing them to be washed out.

A dog must have a sable gene to be a sable. Therefore there must be at least one sable parent to produce a sable puppy. A dog cannot carry the sable gene recessively, which means that two black and tan dogs bred together will never produce a sable puppy.

A homogeneous sable, also called a dominant sable, is a dog that received one sable gene from both of his parents. This means that he carries nothing but sable genes and will only produce sable puppies no matter what female he is bred to. When a sable puppy is born from two sable parents, this does not automatically make the puppy a "dominant sable." This is because the pup could have received the parent's recessive gene rather than their sable gene.

Sable German Shepherds have been around since the very beginning of the breed, and the very first registered German Shepherd Dog was sable in color. The sable color is not very common in the German show lines. They do not generally do well in the SV style show ring. Sable dogs are very common in working lines.

Bicolor

Bicolor shepherds are considered a variation of the black and tan. The dog's entire body is black except for a few areas of brown or tan, usually on the feet, under the tail, in the eyebrows, and sometimes there is a small spot on the cheeks.

Darker black and tans are often advertised incorrectly as bicolor but a true bicolor is very dark with very little color on the body at all. The only way to identify a puppy at birth as a bicolor versus a black is to look for a little bit of brown under their tail.

In some circles there a debate whether bicolor is an actual color or simply a pattern. Regardless, it's known that bicolor is recessive to the typical black and tan patterns such as a saddle back or blanket back, and bicolor dogs will carry another bicolor gene or black gene recessively. Bicolor is the most recessive acceptable color other than solid black.

Bicolor shepherds are not seen in West German show lines but are found in various working lines.

Black

Black German Shepherds can be completely black; they can have a little bit of brown hair on their feet or toes, or a white spot on their chest. If a black puppy has tan under his tail, he will end up being a bicolor. Black German Shepherds are seen less often than black and tan dogs, but black is not "rare" or "special" regardless of what breeders may try to lead you to believe.

Black is the most recessive of the acceptable German Shepherd Dog colors. To produce a black puppy, both parents must be black themselves or carry the black gene recessively. A black puppy can pop up in a litter unexpectedly because the black gene can be passed on recessively for several generations. If the other breeding partner does not carry the black gene there will not be any black puppies, but the recessive gene, can still be passed on to the pups in the litter.

Black German Shepherds are not found in West German show lines. Black shepherds are found in German and European working lines, American show lines and backyard breeders/pet lines.

White

Most everyone has seen a white German Shepherd, but few people realize the controversy white shepherds cause within the breed. According to the German Shepherd Dog breed standard, white is a disqualifying fault and cannot be bred or shown in conformation. The American Kennel Club (AKC) allows white shepherds to be bred and receive registration papers, but they are disqualified from being shown in conformation.

In the GSD breed the white color is actually an absence of color. It is called a masking gene; the dog's true genetic color is masked, making the dog appear white in color. A white GSD has the genetic color of a black and tan, sable, or black but you will not see these colors.

There are breeders and owners who responsibly breed and show their white shepherds under various organizations. The White German Shepherd Dog Club International (WGSDCII) was created to help promote and maintain the white-coated GSD. The American White Shepherd Association (AWSA) was also founded for the recognition and preservation of the White Shepherd in the United States.

The White GSD is called different names in other countries. It's known as the Berger Blanc Swiss dog, White Swiss Shepherd or the American-Canadian White Shepherd.

CHAPTER 4: GERMAN SHEPHERD BLOODLINES – AMERICAN VS. GERMAN

There is a major split between American and German bloodlines within the German Shepherd Dog breed. American bloodlines are shown in AKC (American Kennel Club) conformation. German line dogs do not generally do well in this venue.

German dogs are bred to the WUSV standard, and American dogs are bred to the GSDCA standard. The two standards are similar with just a few variations, and they are interpreted very differently. Between the two lines, a vastly different German Shepherd Dog is created.

Structure and temperament is an important part of the German Shepherd breed. Correct conformation is what helps to ensure the breed continues to look like a German Shepherd Dog. Structure and temperament also helps to ensure the German Shepherd is built and prepared for the type of work intended.

American Show Lines

American show line German Shepherd dogs are bred differently than most other German Shepherd dogs. They are bred solely for the show ring and not for working ability.

Flying Trot

American German Shepherds are bred for what is called the "flying trot." The flying trot is a side gait that is created by extreme angulations in the hind-quarters. Some people refer to this angulation as a "sloped back." Extreme angulations are a controversial topic within the German Shepherd Dog world.

The expectations of an American-bred German Shepherd should be for them to live as a pet or to be shown in AKC confirmation competitions. These German Shepherd dogs are not bred for working ability and are generally not genetically capable of performing police or military duties, search and rescue, Schutzhund, herding, etc.

Beware there is a common misconception that the extreme angulations in American bred German Shepherds causes hip dysplasia. Poor breeding choices by breeders cause hip dysplasia, not angulations.

West German Lines

In Germany, the following minimum requirements for show lines and working lines must be met before breeding:
- BH
- show rating of G (good) or better
- working title (ex: SchH/IPO or HGH)
- passing hip/elbow certification

In addition to the above requirements, most dogs will go on to earn their AD in order to receive their breed survey (Kkl). The breed survey is best obtained before breeding. The breed survey is a requirement before future litters can be given "pink papers," which is the highest registration available and the most sought-after. Dogs are also required to be a minimum age before breeding can begin. Females must be a minimum of 20 months and males are required to be a minimum of 24 months. Line breeding is acceptable but inbreeding is not allowed.

West German Show Lines

West German show line dogs are typically black and red in color and tend to be similar in appearance. Most of these dogs tend to have a saddle back pattern and be large boned. In these lines it is not uncommon to have a long stock coat pup pop up in a litter, or to occasionally run across a lighter sable dog.

West German show line dogs generally thrive in SV/USCA style confirmation shows and do well in Schutzhund. These dogs are also found participating in AKC obedience, agility, herding, and search and rescue. Some are even capable of police and military work.

Some breeders of West German show lines do not care about working ability and only care about (and breed for) winning in the show ring. Fortunately there are others who care about the breed as a whole and breed for a "complete" all-around dog.

West German Working Lines

In addition to the West German show lines, you also have the West German working lines (WGWL). The West German working lines are not as consistent as the West German show lines. Their colors and sizes are more varied. Within these lines you will come across black/tan, black/red, all black, bicolor and sable dogs. Structure can vary from a G (good) show rating to a V (excellent) show rating.

This line is bred more for their working ability and temperament. These dogs are bred to excel at Schutzhund as well as other protection-type sports. You will also find these dogs working as police and military dogs, search and rescue dogs, herding dogs and competing in agility, rally, obedience, or really anything you'd like to train them to do. These German Shepherd dogs are more compact, agile and athletic compared to their show line counterparts.

CHAPTER 5: SELECTING A GERMAN SHEPHERD DOG – PUPPY VS ADULT

Should you get a puppy or an adult? Your heart says puppy but your sensible brain screams adult. Which one will it be? There are positives and negatives to each option and this decision will come down to each individual situation and personal preference.

When starting out with a puppy, you are responsible for raising, training and molding him or her to fit into your family or lifestyle. This can be a positive or a negative. A downside to a puppy is surviving the puppy stage which includes puppy biting, chewing, socialization, and potty training. You also have no guarantee of how a puppy will turn out as an adult. (Stack the odds in your favor by purchasing from a reputable breeder.)

Choosing to go with an older puppy or an adult will give you a better idea of the dog's personality and temperament once it reaches maturity. Depending on the dog, you may be able to determine how it is with children, other dogs, cats, etc., and it may even already be potty trained, crate trained, and have some obedience.

Adult dogs can make wonderful companions, but be aware that you may not know the dog's background, health or temperament issues, and what type of training (if any) the dog has been through. An adult German Shepherd may require some time to adjust and bond with you and your family.

Purchasing a puppy may be the best choice if you have young children and are hesitant to bring an adult dog into your household. Some people like the puppy stage and prefer to raise the dog from the beginning. However, if you have a hectic lifestyle and are unsure if you can devote your time to a puppy, an adult dog may be the best option for r you.

CHAPTER 6: SELECTING A GERMAN SHEPHERD DOG – MALES VS. FEMALE

Male or female-which gender is right for you? Let's look at the difference between male and female German Shepherd dogs.

There are theories and opinions that females are more protective but easier to train and that males are more aggressive, territorial and stubborn, but more affectionate.

These theories really boil down to an individual's personal preference or past experiences, the breed, and the individual dog and its unique personality. Genetics, a dog's pedigree, training and environment can also play a role in how stubborn, easy to train or aggressive a dog may or may not be.

For every male versus female theory, you can find just as many German Shepherd dogs that prove the opposite.

The one characteristic that is generally true for each gender is size. Males are usually going to be larger than females, making male German Shepherds stronger and more difficult to handle. It is much easier to physically control a sixty pound female than it is to hold the leash to an eighty-five pound male.

Do not forget to consider the most obvious gender differences. A female will come into heat if left intact. If you do not plan on breeding your female, you will need to take preventative measures during her heat cycle to prevent an unwanted pregnancy or look into spaying as a permanent solution. An intact male has higher testosterone levels, which increase his aggression and creates more territorial behavior. Intact males tend to "mark" their territory more than neutered males. It can also become difficult to live with an intact male if there are females in heat nearby.

If you are unsure which gender you would prefer, talk to a breeder about your family structure, environment, and what you are looking for in your new pet. A good breeder will help match you with the best puppy suited for you.

If you already have a dog and will be adding a second one to your pack structure, you should consider going with the opposite sex of what you already have. This will eliminate any same sex aggression issues that can occur and become a problem.

CHAPTER 7: SELECTING A GERMAN SHEPHERD DOG – BREEDER VS. RESCUE

So you have decided you want to add a German Shepherd to your household. You will next need to determine where your German Shepherd Dog will come from. The two most common options are buying from a breeder or going through a rescue organization. There are pros and cons to both.

Breeder

A good breeder will do everything within his or her power to produce healthy puppies that will be free of genetic health disorders. You will also have the advantage of knowing your dog's bloodlines and genetic health history. Good breeders want the best for their pups and will offer you lifetime help and support, should you need it. A good breeder will also be knowledgeable of their lines and can help you with things to watch for as your pup grows and matures.

Buying from a breeder usually costs more. Many breeders also have a screening process that all potential buyers must go through (and pass) in order to purchase from them.

Rescue

Getting a dog from a rescue organization will cost far less than a dog from a breeder. Rescue dogs are usually current on vaccines, vet care, and may even be spayed or neutered. Getting a dog from a rescue organization can be very rewarding. You know you have saved a dog's life and made a difference.

Many rescues also have a screening process to ensure that you and your home are a good match for the dog. The screening process can be tough, so be prepared.

The negative to rescuing a dog is that you'll rarely receive any background information. The odds are high that rescue dogs are a product of irresponsible breeders or owners. With that being said, you roll the dice with any dog you bring into your home and allow into your heart.

If you do not care about bloodlines or pedigrees and are simply looking for a companion, rescue is an option. If you are interested in sport or working activities with your German Shepherd, it is recommended that you consider a dog from a quality breeder.

Be aware that German Shepherds go quickly in rescues and shelters. Diligence, patience and a bit of luck may be needed if you choose to go this route.

CHAPTER 8: DISTINGUSIGHING GOOD BREEDERS FROM BAD

The renowned traits that make the German Shepherd a great dog are what draw people to the breed. Traits like stable temperament, striking appearance, intelligence, loyalty, and courage. Regardless of your plans or personal goals for your new family member, you want to make sure your German Shepherd acts and looks like a German Shepherd and has the best odds to live a long and healthy life.

All German Shepherds have the potential to be great dogs. Well-breed German Shepherds have the potential to be even greater than others. Finding a good breeder can be a challenge, and if you are new to the German Shepherd breed it may be hard to distinguish the good breeders from the bad.

Be prepared with this list:

12 Questions To Ask The Breeder

1. AKC registered?
- The answer to this question should never be no if you are in the United States. If their dogs are not AKC registered, keep looking.

2. Parent's hip and elbow certified?
- Both parents need to be hip and elbow certified and the breeder should be willing to provide proof of this. If proof cannot be provided, keep looking.

3. What working titles do the parents have? The bloodline have?
- Titles help ensure dogs have been tested and are breed worthy. This may or may not be a deal-breaker for some people.

4. Do you own one or both of the parents?

- Breeders usually own the female and sometimes own the male. Ask to see and/or interact with the parents.

5. What is the puppy's environment?

- Where are the puppies kept and raised? Good breeders whelp and keep puppies in a well-thought out and designated area. Some breeders even keep the puppies inside the house until they get older and are harder to manage. If a breeder keeps the puppies unrestricted in their backyard, keep looking.

6. At what age do your puppies go to their new homes?

- 8 weeks is standard for a puppy to go to its new home. Some breeders may let a puppy go to an experienced home at 7 weeks. If a breeder routinely sends puppies' home at 6 weeks, keep looking.

7. What type of socialization and interaction has taken place with the puppies?

- You want to look for a breeder who has lots of interaction with their puppies and socializes their litter with as many things and people as possible. The more a breeder does with their puppies during the first eight weeks, the better start your puppy will have.

8. What do the puppies come with? (Vaccinations, micro chipped, tattooed, etc.)

- Reputable breeders send their puppies to their new homes as healthy as possible. Some breeder's micro chip or tattoo their puppies for identification purposes.

9. Purchase price?

- You won't know if you don't ask. A good pet quality puppy will run from $800 to $2,000. A good working quality puppy will start at off around $1,500 and go up from there. The more titles the parents and the bloodline have, the more expensive the puppy will be.

10. Do you have a buyer screening process?

- Good breeders will screen the buyers of their puppies to ensure that the right puppy goes to the right home. Some breeders have a formal application process and others verbally screen potential buyers.

11. Do you have a contract and a health guarantee?

- Contracts and guarantees can vary a great deal. Be sure that you read the contract, understand the health guarantee and are comfortable with all aspects of the details. If you run across a breeder who does not offer a contract or a health guarantee, keep looking.

12. What is your role after the puppies leave your care?

- Good breeders care about their puppies and will want to be updated on achievements or major health issues. A good breeder is a valuable resource who will offer advice and any necessary help throughout your dog's life.

Tips To Spotting A Backyard Breeder

A backyard breeder is someone who is breeding irresponsibly for the wrong reasons. Backyard breeders are not trying to improve the German Shepherd Dog as a breed. They are usually breeding just to make money. Backyard breeders usually have untitled dogs from undesirable pedigrees and do no health or temperament testing.

Backyard breeders do not care what happens to their puppies once they have left their yards. They simply want your money and to never hear from you again. Many of these backyard breeders have a good sales pitch and advertise that their dogs are family members raised in the house.

A puppy from a backyard breeder will cost considerably less ($300 to $600) than a well-bred puppy from a reputable breeder. You will save money on the purchase price from a backyard breeder, but will end up paying more in the long run for vet bills due to genetic problems, not to mention the heartache felt from your friend's suffering. The old saying "you get what you pay for" holds true. Pay the higher price for a well-bred puppy. You are not only buying health but peace of mind and lifetime breeder support.

A backyard breeder may seem credible at first glance, but once you ask the 12 questions, the truth will be quickly revealed.

CHAPTER 9: MAINTNANCE & HEALTH CONCERNS

All breeds require maintenance care and have pre disposed and breed-specific health issues. No breed (and no dog) is perfect.

When it comes to grooming, the German Shepherd Dog is a wash and wear, low-maintenance breed.

Grooming the German "Shedder"

Shedding – German Shepherds shed, a lot. Over the years I have had a total of four indoor German Shepherds and regardless of their coat types, they all shed. German Shepherds shed year-round and "blow" their coat twice a year.

If you cannot tolerate dust bunnies in your house and are finicky about dog hair on your clothes, furniture and everywhere in your vehicle, you need to rethink owning a German Shepherd.

Brushing – Brushing your German Shepherd regularly is important to keep their coats clean, healthy and help reduce shedding. A quick brushing on a daily basis is ideal if possible, but German Shepherds need a thorough brushing at least once per week. German Shepherds with longer coats may require brushing on a more frequent basis.

Regularly brushing your German Shepherd will prevent matting of the undercoat and potential skin problems such as hotspots, bald spots and rashes.

I use and recommend the FURminator. The product claims to reduce shedding up to 90% and it is the best brush I have ever used. Only light pressure needs to be applied when brushing and the amount of hair it removes is mind-blowing. Search for the product on Amazon and Ebay to find it much cheaper than in retail pet stores.

Bathing – The German Shepherd Dog has a low-maintenance coat and should ideally be bathed only once or twice per year to prevent drying out their skin. Over-bathing your shepherd will strip its coat of its natural oils. Always use shampoo made for dogs and be careful to avoid soap and water in their eyes and ears.

Toes – Check your German Shepherd's nails regularly and keep them trimmed. Just like people, some dog's nails grow faster than others. Split or broken nails are often the result of nails that have been allowed to grow too long.

Nail trimmers can be purchased from your vet or local pet store. Trim off small amounts of the nail a little bit at a time to avoid cutting the "quick" in the nail. (The quick is a small vein in the nail) If you cut your dog's nail to short and cut into the quick this is painful for your dog and causes the nail to bleed. Styptic powder or cornstarch pressed firmly into the bleeding nail will stop the bleeding. Styptic powder can be purchased at your favorite pet store. You need to have it accessible BEFORE you begin trimming nails. Cutting nails too short happens from time to time, so it is best to be prepared.

Coated German Shepherds and plush coats may have tuffs of hair between their toes and excessive hair that grows between the pads on the bottom of their feet. This extra hair can be trimmed and maintained with scissors or dog shears.

Dental Health – Proper dental care is an important part of your shepherd's maintenance routine. Preventative care for your shepherd's pearly whites will improve his overall health and may save you lots of money over the span of your dog's lifetime.

The danger of dental disease in dogs is often overlooked, but it can be very serious. Plaque builds up on the teeth and turns into tartar. (Plaque begins to turn into tartar within 24 to 48 hours.) Tartar is where bacteria grows, and over time starts to eat away at the teeth and gums. Bacteria is the cause of bad breath, oral pain, periodontal disease and tooth loss. Bacteria in the mouth can travel through your dog's system and affect other parts of the body.

Prevent dental disease in your German Shepherd by starting a dental care routine as soon as possible. Brush your shepherd's teeth regularly (daily brushing is recommended) using a finger brush or a toothbrush designed for dogs along with enzymatic doggy toothpaste. Start out by letting your shepherd smell and lick the toothbrush and toothpaste and ease into the actual brushing. Gently brush your dog's teeth and don't forget to get in and around the gum line.

Dry dog food is healthier for your shepherd's teeth and gums verses wet or semi-moist food. The hard food helps scrape away plaque from the teeth and gums. Hard rubber toys and other items designed for chewing assist in keeping gums healthy and keeps plaque from lingering on teeth. Oral rinses designed for dogs and dental treats are also good to add into your shepherd's dental routine, but regular brushing is your best preventive measure against dental disease.

If you think your shepherd is experiencing dental discomfort or pain, contact your veterinarian for a routine dental exam immediately.

Symptoms of potential dental problems:

- Red or swollen gums
- Bleeding gums
- Increased salivation
- Bad breath
- Reluctance to chew
- Missing or loose teeth
- Tarter – brown or yellow coating on teeth resulting from plaque build-up

Eyes – The German Shepherd breed is not plagued with eye abnormalities that require constant cleaning nor do they have protruding eyes that can be prone to injury. Overall, the shepherd's eyes don't require much attention.

With that, general eye irritations can occur in any breed ranging from contact with pollens in the air to sharp objects, such as the tip of a foxtail. Most eye irritations are not serious and go away on their own within a few days.

Symptoms of irritated eyes include the following:

- Red, itchy eyes
- Watery eyes
- Yellow or green discharge in the corner of the eye
- Inflamed skin around the eye
- Squinting or reluctance to open the eye

Irritated eyes are usually easy to treat but it is recommended that you let your veterinarian determine if your German Shepherd's eye irritation is minor or more serious.

Pannus (Chronic Superficial Keratitis) is an eye condition that is seen primarily in the German Shepherd breed and is believed to be caused from genetics. Symptoms usually occur between the ages of three and six and sometimes even earlier. If the corneas of your shepherd's eyes look discolored or milky, make an appointment with your veterinarian immediately.

The condition is an autoimmune disease that slowly and gradually attacks the cornea of the eye, and it affects your shepherd's vision. If Pannus is left untreated it may eventually lead to blindness.

Your veterinarian can prescribe medications to slow down the degenerative process and keep your shepherd's eyes comfortable and pain free.

Ears – German Shepherds have erect, open ears. The benefit to open ears is the increased air circulation in the ear canal.

Maintaining healthy ears in your German Shepherd is easy through prevention. Check your shepherd's ears weekly and clean them as necessary. Products can be purchased from your vet or local pet store to clean excess wax and dirt. Never use Q-Tips or alcohol to clean your German Shepherd's ears.

Ear infections can occur if a foreign object invades the ear canal, if water becomes trapped in the ear canal, or they can be caused by allergies.

Here are some common indicators that a trip to your local veterinarian is necessary:

- Ears are sensitive to touch
- Head shaking
- Ear scratching
- Skin redness inside the ears
- Swelling
- Discharge or blood in the ear
- Unpleasant odor coming from the ear
- Hematomas (blood blisters) on the ear flap
- Melanomas (tumors)

Health Concerns

Like a lot of popular pedigree breeds, the German Shepherd Dog is susceptible to certain hereditary conditions and health issues. Purchasing your German Shepherd from a reputable breeder who offers a health guarantee will reduce the chances of health issues over the span of your pet's life, but there is unknown risk regardless of the dog or breed. Future and current German Shepherd owners need to be aware of health concerns that are prevalent in this breed.

Arthritis – Many German Shepherds develop some form of joint disease and arthritis that is not uncommon due to the breed's large size. The majority of canine arthritis cases fall somewhere between mild and causing complete lameness. Many options are available for treating arthritis in your German Shepherd.

Bloat – Also known as gastric dilation/volvulus, gastric torsion and twisted gut. (This is a life-threatening condition that has become more common in deep-chested dogs over the years.) The stomach swells from a rapid accumulation of air and requires immediate veterinary care. Bloat is considered by some to be the second leading cause of death after cancer among large and giant breed dogs.

Cancer – The most serious disease affecting any breed is cancer. The German Shepherd is susceptible to various types of cancer:
- Osteosarcoma - Bone cancer, with tumors that most commonly occur in the limbs (elbow or knee area)
- Lymphoma – Cancer that affects the lymphoid system
- Hemangiosarcoma – Cancer that originates in the vascular endothelial cells that line the capillaries
- Melanoma – Cancer formed from small cells resulting in pigment within the skin

Regular veterinary check-ups increase the likelihood tumors and symptoms will be detected early so that they can be treated.

Degenerative Myelopathy – A neurological disease that is a slow, progressive paralysis of the dog's hind legs. This disease generally starts in late middle age and
eventually the dog cannot walk on its own. There is no cure. This disease is very similar to Multiple Sclerosis in humans. A simple and inexpensive saliva DNA test can be performed in the comfort of your home and will determine if your shepherd is normal, a carrier, or at risk.

Epilepsy – A chronic condition characterized by recurrent seizures. The cause of seizures in German Shepherds can be the result of head trauma, brain tumors, liver disease, low blood sugar, severe worm infestation, genetic factors, kidney failure, vitamin deficiencies, cancers, etc.

Watching a beloved pet in the throes of a seizure is a horrifying experience, but it can be successfully controlled with medication.

Heart Disease – Like many large breeds, German Shepherds can suffer from murmurs, valve disease and enlarged hearts.

Hip & Elbow Dysplasia – The most common hereditary condition in the German Shepherd breed. Dysplasia is the most common heritable orthopedic disease in large and giant dog breeds. Dysplasia is caused when a looseness occurs in the joint. The loose joint usually leads to degenerative joint disease and arthritis. These symptoms reduce the range of motion in the affected joints and causes pain and inflammation.

Pancreatic Insufficiency – The dog is unable to digest food properly, resulting in an excessive appetite while becoming increasingly thin. Treatment is life-long and requires pancreatic enzymes to be administered with food.

Panosteitis – Most commonly referred to as "Pano" it literally means inflammation of all bones. It usually occurs between the ages of 6 to 18 months and the symptoms are lameness or limping. Pano comes and goes from day-to-day and changes from leg to leg. Pano is not a result of trauma or injury and is often referred to as "growing pains." Males are more prone to pano then females.

I had a male puppy who suffered from pano off and on for over a year. I treated his flare-ups with anti-inflammatory medication and reduced his activity level as much as possible.

Von Willebrand's Disease – An inherited bleeding disorder. Excessive bleeding occurs following an injury or spontaneous hemorrhage (nose bleed) due to the lack of glycoprotein in the blood needed for clotting.

Purchasing a German Shepherd Dog from a reputable breeder and knowing what questions to ask will significantly increase the odds of raising a genetically healthy German Shepherd.

CHAPTER 10: FUN FACTS

The first German Shepherd Dog set paw on upon North American soil in 1906.

The first German Shepherd Dog was exhibited in America in 1907.

The first German Shepherd was registered with the AKC in 1908.

In the United States, the correct name of the breed is German Shepherd Dog (GSD). This breed is commonly referred to by the acronym GSD. The German Shepherd is the only breed to have the word "dog" as part of its full name.

German Shepherds are one of the most registered dogs, which proves their popularity as a breed.

German Shepherds are the third most popular breed in the U.S.

Stanley Coren, author of *"The Intelligence of Dogs,"* ranked the German Shepherd as the third most intelligent species of dog.

The average size of a German Shepherd litter is 8 puppies.

What does your dog say about you? People who own herding dogs like German Shepherds tend to be more extroverted.

The German Shepherd is the first breed to be trained as a working guide dog.
- In 1928 "Buddy" became the first Seeing Eye dog.
- Helen Keller owned German Shepherds.

Strongheart, a male German Shepherd, was one of the earliest canine film stars and a popular celebrity in his day
- Stongheart paved the way for Rin Tin Tin.

- Strongheart has a star on the Hollywood Walk of Fame located at 1724 Vine Street.
- Strongheart Dog Food was named after Strongheart and is still produced.

Rin Tin Tin is a famous German Shepherd who made 26 movies in 14 years for Warner Brothers.

- Rin Tin Tin has a star on the Hollywood Walk of Fame located at 1623 Vine Street.
- Greta Garbo, Jean Harlow, and W.K. Kellogg each owned a descendant of Rin Tin Tin.
- The first Rin Tin Tin died in the arms of Jean Harlow in 1932. She allegedly came running when she heard that her favorite neighborhood dog was ill.

Original Rin Tin Tin 1929

Bullet the Wonder Dog was a male German Shepherd who appeared on *The Roy Rogers Show,* a television series (1951–1957). Bullet was also the family pet and belonged to the show's married stars, Roy Rogers and Dale Evans.

Jack LeLanne's white German Shepherd made regular appearances on LeLanne's daily fitness show in the 1950s.

Maxmillian was a black and tan male German Shepherd who was introduced into *The "Bionic Woman"* in 1977 (episode 45). Max had a bionic jaw and bionic legs.

Franklin Delano Roosevelt owned a German Shepherd named Major when he moved into the White House.

President John Kennedy had a German Shepherd, named "Clipper" who was known to be a strong protector of Jackie. When the press asked what he ate, Jackie replied, "Reporters."

The Kennedy Clan 1963

Vice President Joe Biden's German Shepherd Champ, named by his grandchildren, resides with him.

CHAPTER 11: ACRONYMS, TERMS & TITLES

Acronyms & Terms

AKC - American Kennel Club

CKC - Canadian Kennel Club

CKC - Continental Kennel Club (not to be confused with the Canadian Kennel Club)

DHV: Deutscher Hundesport Verein – German Dog Sport Club

DM - Degenerative Myelopathy

GSD - German Shepherd Dog

GSDCA - German Shepherd Dog Club of America

GSDCA-WDA - German Shepherd Dog Club of America – Working Dog Association

GSDCC – German Shepherd Dog Club of Canada

GSSCC - German Shepherd Schutzhund Club of Canada

KC – Kennel Club (Great Britain)

SAR - Search and Rescue

SV: SV Verein für Deutsche Schäferhunde - (German   Shepherd Dog Club) The original GSD breed club and breed registry, based in Germany.

UKC – United Kennel Club

USA - United Schutzhund Clubs of America

vWD Normal - Rating of test for von Willebrand's disease

WGSL - West German Show Lines

WUSV - World Union of SVs

Breeding Definitions

Inbreeding – A deliberate breeding where the Sire and Dam are directly related.

Linebreeding – A breeding where the Sire and Dam have one or more direct ancestor generally in the second or third generation of the pedigree. This is the most common type of breeding that occurs.

Outcrossing – Breeding where the sire and dam have no obvious ancestors. Generally used to infuse a line with stronger traits or to add a desired genetic base or type.

Pedigree – A family tree - traces the animal's related ancestors, usually to the fourth generation.

Hip & Elbow Certifications

"a" stamp Zuerkannt - German certification hips that fall within the following 3 categories:
1. "a" normal - Certified normal hips
2. "a" fast normal - Certified near normal hips
3. "a" Noch Zugelassen - Certified still permissible hips

PennHip – The procedure measures hip joint laxity; it does not grade a passing or failing score. Loose hips are more prone to develop degenerative joint disease. The procedure was developed at University of Pennsylvania (USA).

OFA - Orthopedic Foundation of America
OFA – Hips are rated within the following 3 catagories:
1. Normal – Excellent rated better than Good
2. Transitional – Fair rated better than Borderline
3. Dysplastic – Mild rated better than Moderate and both rated better than Severe

OFA elbow certification is rated either Normal or Dysplastic

Titles

AOE: Award of Excellence – dog must have OFA certified hips and elbows, have a recognized working title, and be temperament certified.

BIS – Best in Show

BOB – Best of Breed

BP – Best Puppy (of breed)

BPIS - Best Puppy in Show (best puppy of all breeds at an all-breed show)

CD – Companion Dog

CDX - Companion Dog Excellent

CH - Champion of Confirmation in AKC or CKC

Gebrauchshundklasse: Working Dog Class – The only class available for animals over two.

Grand Victor/Grand Victrix - Best male and female at the German Shepherd Dog Club of America National Specialty Show each year

Group I, II, III, & IV – Ranking in Herding Group competition at all breed shows.

GV/GVX – Grand Victor/Grand Victrix

HC - Herding Champion

HIT – High in Trial

HGH: Herdengebrauchshund - Herding Dog. A qualificationof dogs working with flocks

HT - Herding Tested

INT: Internationale Prufungsklasse – International Training Degree

Kr.H: Krigshund – War Dog

M.H: Militar hund – Military Dog

NOC – National Obedience Champion

OTCh – Obedience Trial Champion

OV: Obedience Victor (male) or Victrix (female) – the top Obedience dog at the National Specialty Show. The dog must have no disqualifying faults and must earn the top combined score in the trial.

ROM/ROMC - Register of merit awarded to sires and dams based on achievements of offspring (ROM is based on AKC; ROMC is based on CKC).

S.H.: Sanitats hund – Red Cross Dog

TD - Tracking Dog

TSB: Triebveranlagung – Fighting Drive

UD: Utility Dog – Working Qualification

UDX - Utility Dog Excellent

VCD1, 2, 3, & 4 – Versatile Companion Dog

VCCH - Versatile Companion Champion

SV Titles

A: Ausreichend – sufficient show or performance rating

AD: Aus Dauerprufing – German Endurance Test

B or BH: Begleithunde – Basic Companion Dog. The preliminary requirement for dogs working towards Schutzhund titles. A combination temperament and obedience test. B and BH are used interchangeably.

BIH: Blindenhund – Guide Dog for the Blind

BPA: Bundessiegerprüfung – German National Working Show

BpDH I, II: Bahnpolizeidiensthund - Railroad Police Service Dog

Bundesleistungssieger – German National Working Dog Champion

Bundeszuchtsieger – Confirmation winner at the German National All-Breed show

DH: Diensthund – Service Dog

DPH: Dienstpolizeihund – Service Police Dog

FH I, II, & III: Fahrtenhund – Tracking titles level 1 - 3

G: Gut - good show or performance rating

GrH: Grenzenhund – Border Patrol Dog

HGH: Herdengebrauchshund – Herding Utility Dog

Hutesieger – Champion Herding Dog

IPO I, II, III - International Schutzhund degrees with increasing levels of difficulty combining tracking, obedience and protection.

Junghundsieger – Young class winner (12 -18 months) at the Sieger show

KKLI: Körklasse 1 – recommended for breeding by the SV

KKLII: Körklasse 2 – rated suitable for breeding by the SV

KNVP - Ring Sport. Also known as the Royal Dutch Police Dog Sport that began in Holland in the early 1900s

Körung - Breed Survery

Landessieger – Winner at the Regional SchH III competition

LawH: Lawinen Hund – Avalanhce Rescue Dog

Lbz: Lebenszeit – breed surveyed for life

M: Mangelhaft – faulty show or performance rating

PFP I,II: Polizeifahrtenhund – Police Tracking Dog

PH: Polizeihund – Police Dog

PSP I, II: Polizei-Schutzhundprüfung – Police Protection Dog

SchHA: Schutzhundprüfung - Limited SchH Title – Similar to SchH 1 but without the tracking portion

SchH I, II, III: Schutzhundprüfung 1 (novice), 2 (intermediate), 3 (master level) - Increasing levels of Schutzhund degrees combining tracking, obedience and protection.

SG: Sehr Gut – very good show or performance rating

Sieger/Siegerin – Grand Victor/Victrix at the National Sieger show (VA-1)

U: Ungenugend – insufficient show or performance rating

V: Vorzüglich – excellent show or performance rating

VA: Vorzüglich – Auslese – Excellent Select sho rating given only at Sieger show

VH: Vorhanden – sufficient show or performance rating

WH – Schutzhund title related to protection work

ZH I, II: Zollhund – Customs Police Dog

Temperament Titles

BH – German Companion Dog (SV)

CGC – Canine Good Citizen (AKC)

TC – Temperament Certificate (awarded by the GSDCA)

TDI – Therapy Dog International Certification (TDI)

TT – Temperament Tested (awarded by the American Temperament Test Society)

CHAPTER 12: HELPFUL RESOURCES

Organizations

American Kennel Club (AKC)
www.akc.org

American White Shepherd Association
www.awsaclub.com

Association of Pet Dog Trainers (APDT)
www.apdt.com

British Association for German Shepherd Dogs
www.bagsd.com

Canadian Kennel Club (CKO)
www.ckc.ca

Canine Companions for Independence
www.caninecompanions.org

German Shepherd Dog Club of America (GSDCA)
www.gsdca.org

German Shepherd Dog Club of America–Working Dog Association
www.gsdca-wda.org

Herding on the Web
www.herdingontheweb.com

International Agility Link (IAL)
www.agilityclick.com

North American Dog Agility Council (NADAC)
http://www.nadac.com/

North American Flyball Association (FAFA)
www.flyball.org

North American Police Work Dog Association
www.napwda.com

Orthopedic Foundation for Animals
www.offa.org

PennHip
www.vet.upenn.edu/pennhip

Pet Partners
www.petpartners.org

The Kennel Club (UK)
www.the-kennel-club.org.uk

United Kennel Club (UKO)
www.ukcdogs.com

United Schutzhund Clubs of America
www.germanshepherddog.com

United States Dog Agility Association (USDAA)
http://www.usdaa.com

Verein fur Deutsche Schaferhunde (SV)
http://www.schaeferhunde.de

White German Shepherd Dog Club International, Inc.
www.whitegermanshepherd.org

White German Shepherd Dog Club of America (WGSDCA)
www.wgsdca.org

World Canine Freestyle Organization
www.worldcaninefreestyle.org

Magazines

AKC Family dog
www.akc.org/pubs/familydog

Clean Run (Agility)
http://www.cleanrun.com

Dog & Kennel
www.dogandkennel.com

Dog Fancy
www.dogfancy.com

Dog World Magazine
www.dogworldmag.com

The German Shepherd Quarterly
http://www.hoflin.com/Magazines/The_German_Shepherd_Qrtly

Working Dogs Cyberzine
www.workingdogs.com

Animal Welfare Groups and Rescue Organizations

American German Shepherd Rescue Association, Inc.
www.agsra.com

American Humane Association (AHA)
www.aspca.org

Royal Society for the Prevention of Cruelty to Animals (RSPCA)
www.rspca.org.uk

The Humane Society of the United States (HSUS)
www.hsus.org

World Animal Net (UK)
www.worldanimal.net

Veterinary Resources

American Academy of Veterinary Acupuncture (AAVA)
www.aava.org

American Animal Hospital Association (AAHA)
www.aahanet.org

American College of Veterinary Ophthalmologists (ACVO)
www.acvo.com

American Veterinary Chiropractic Association (AVCA)
www.animalchiropractic.org

American Veterinary Medical Association (AVMA)
www.avma.org

British Veterinary Association (BVA)
www.bva.co.uk

MEET THE AUTHOR

Amy & Cozmo

Amy Morford has over twenty years of dog training experience with companion dogs, sport dogs and working breeds. Amy's motivation to write about dogs stems from her love for them and their unbiased loyalty and devotion. Amy's goal is to provide helpful, accurate information to assist dog lovers with raising and training a well-mannered, good-tempered, happy, healthy, well-adjusted companion, friend, partner and/or family pet.

Check out **DogTrainingPlace.Net** for dog training tips and over 10,000 name ideas.

OTHER BOOKS AND PRODUCTS BY AMY

DoggyPedia: All You Need To Know About Dogs

Dog Eldercare: Caring For Your Middle-Aged To Older Dog (Dog Care for the Older Canine)

Dog Quotes: Proverbs, Quotes & Quips

How to Speak Dog: Dog Training Simplified For Dog Owners

Pet Names and Numerology: Choose the Right Name For Your Pet

Puppy Training: From Day 1 to Adulthood (How to Make Your Puppy Loving and Obedient)

Scared Dog Audio

Made in the USA
Lexington, KY
31 October 2013